Sugartopia

ISBN: 978-1-950817-14-6 (Paperback)
ISBN: 978-1-950817-13-9 (Hardcover)

Any references to historical events, real people, or real places, are used fictitiously.
Names, characters, and places are products of the author's imagination.

Front cover image by Milena Matić.

Printed by Power Corner Press, in the United States of America

First printing edition 2020.

Power Corner Press
1360 University Ave W Ste #351
Saint Paul, MN, 55104

www.powercornerpress.com

Baby Daisy

💕 For A'meria Z. 💕

July 21, 1999 — May 29, 2005

The skies are dark grey,
the rain how it pours,
it's way too stormy to play outdoors.

But Mari and Ella are quite content,
reading with flashlights in their blanket tent.

They fall asleep and when they awake,
they find their world filled with candy and cake.

"Sugartopia" reads the candy cane sign.
It's covered with sprinkles and licorice vines.

As they explore,
the girls meet someone new.

A girl with a halo
dressed in glittery blue.

Her name is A'meria, she says, "Hello!"
There's something about her the girls do not know.

She shows them around and gives them a snack.
They race up and down a green taffy track.

Together they play in the warm golden sun.
In Sugartopia every day's fun.

On a hill, they discover three candy balls,
bigger than big and taller than tall.

Excited to see them,
they climb up on top

Then roll down the hill
unable to stop.

They crash right into
a jellybean tree.

The trunk falls open.
Guess what they see?

Inside are some sour
blueberry guitars.

The girls jam together and rock out like stars.

A'meria says, "Let's go for a ride!"
She leads them to a lake
with a twist-y slide.

They jump right into the chocolate-y waters.

Splash, giggle and squeal like three muddy otters.

While they are swimming, they hear a weird sound,
Candy unicorns and dragons are prancing around.

The girls get out of the water,
let the animals drink.

When they pet them, their hands get covered in pink.

Soon Mari and Ella shut their sleepy eyes,
With their new friend, A'meria, watching nearby.

They fall asleep soundly and have candy dreams,
Among bright orangesicles and strawberry cream.

At their grandparents' house, the two girls awake,
They tell them about the land of candy and cake.

They tell of the music, the swimming, the race.
And how thrilled they were to be in that place.

Later, Mari notices
something quite small.

A picture of the girl
they met on the wall.

The girl who showed them around candy paradise
Looked out from the picture with sparkling eyes.

Mari and Ella ask, "Who can this be?"
It's their cousin in heaven, A'meria Z.

They'll always remember where they roamed free and proud,
and smile when they think of the little girl in the clouds.

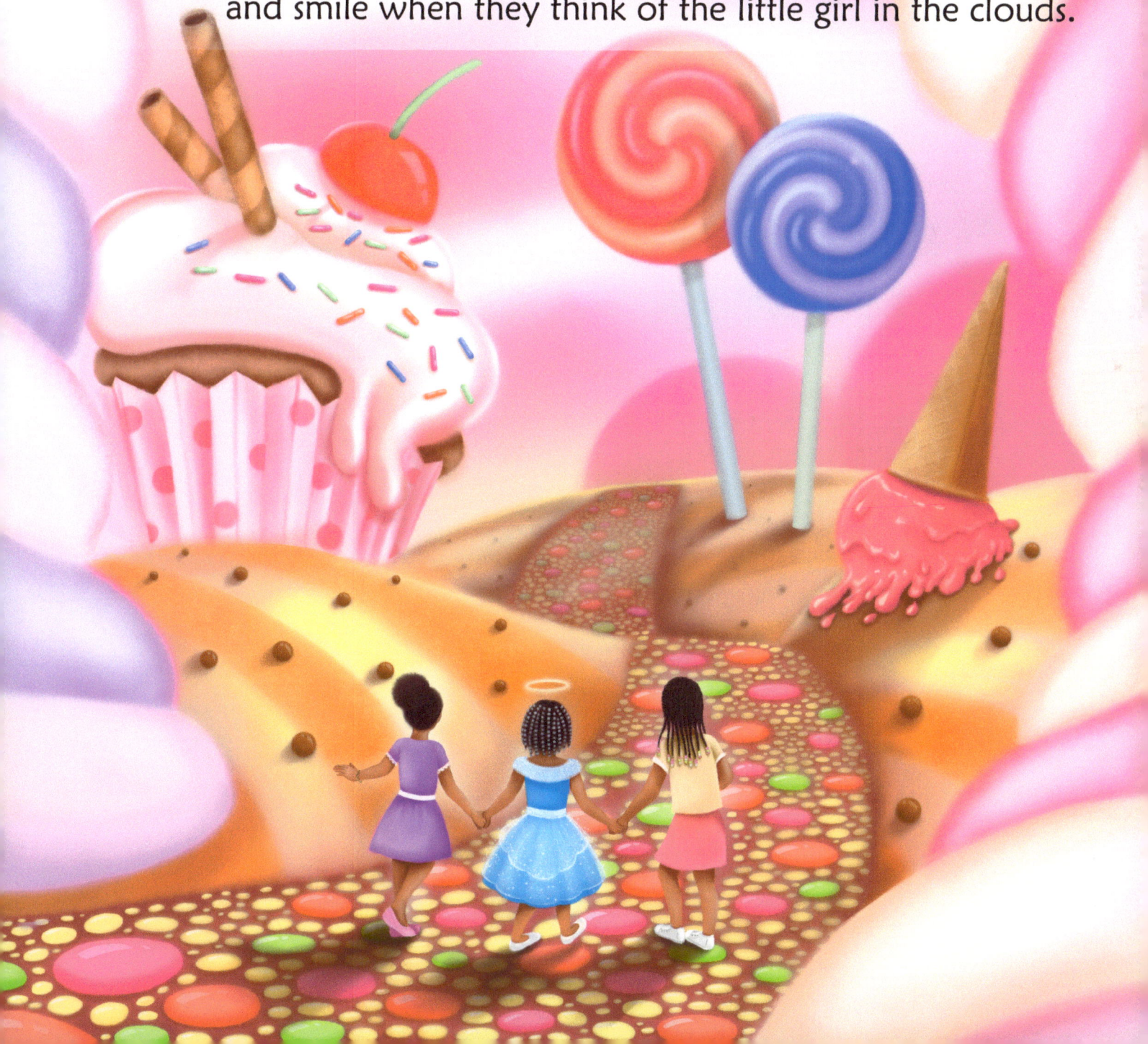

www.ingramcontent.com/pod-product-compliance
Lightning Source LLC
Chambersburg PA
CBHW042118040426
42449CB00002B/96

9781950817146